1

HYMNS
FOR TODAY

Purchased by Jean Chandler

100
HYMNS
FOR TODAY

A SUPPLEMENT TO
Hymns Ancient and Modern

HYMNS ANCIENT & MODERN LIMITED

Cover design by John Piper

MELODY EDITION
ISBN 0 907547 26 5

First published 1969
Twenty-first impression 1985

© Compilation, *Hymns Ancient and Modern Limited*

PRINTED AND BOUND IN GREAT BRITAIN
BY SPOTTISWOODE BALLANTYNE LIMITED
COLCHESTER AND LONDON

PREFACE

Today's Christians need today's songs to sing as well as yesterday's. The great hymns of the past need no patronage or recommendation. But we cannot live only on the achievements of the past. A collection of hymns has to be both modern and ancient if it is genuinely to express the full mind of the people of God. The present volume is in origin a supplement to *Hymns Ancient and Modern Revised* (1950). Accordingly none of its hundred hymns appears in that volume. About forty will probably be new to worshippers of all traditions. The remainder have been gathered from many books in course of a long search for hymns that speak to today.

Although this book is a collection of hymns for our own time, it does not go so far in the direction of modernity as to include those written in an idiom likely to be so shortlived that any book containing them will be dated within months of publication. We have tried to steer a middle course, therefore, between restatements of the traditional and ephemeral or 'pop' productions. On the other hand, the book includes words by older writers such as John Clare, Philip Doddridge, Samuel Wolcott, and Charles Wesley as well as Sydney Carter, Patrick Appleford, Fred Kaan, and other writers of our time. Accordingly, the volume both experiments with some of the hymns of today and seeks to fill gaps in *Hymns Ancient and Modern Revised*.

The book does not assume, as older hymnbooks did, a society more agricultural than industrial, untroubled by questions of race relations and human rights. Nor does it presuppose a church untouched by the fierce conflicts of the century.

The book contains a number of tunes which appear here for the first time. But by deliberate policy the musical editors have not hesitated to use existing and well known tunes. For various reasons, new words have been more difficult to find. The vocabulary and idiom of words used in liturgy and worship become limited by familiar associations. To try and say something wholly fresh is therefore to run the risk of sounding bizarre, if not grotesque. Then there is the fact that the metres and rhymes of an older age are no longer employed by modern poets. Finally, there is an inherent nature of religious language. Hymns tend towards aspiration and interjection. They have never easily endured clear and precise propositional statement. Yet a good Christian hymn will always say something coherent, and will not merely express passing feelings and momentary attitudes. At a time of search for new ways of expressing Christian faith, it is not easy to carry out these explorations within the limits imposed by the form of a hymn. However, the new hymns contained in this volume have seemed to stand out by their quality, and the editors are confident that their presence here will be warmly welcomed by many users.

JOHN DYKES BOWER
GERALD H. KNIGHT
EDGAR BISHOP
CYRIL TAYLOR
HENRY CHADWICK

ACKNOWLEDGEMENTS

Hymns Ancient and Modern Limited thank the owners or controllers of
copyright for permission to use the hymns and tunes listed below. An
asterisk denotes that the text has been altered by permission.

WORDS

AUTHOR	PERMISSION GRANTED BY	NO. OF HYMN
Ambrose, G.	The Society of the Sacred Mission	9
Appleford, P.	Josef Weinberger, Ltd. (from *20th Century Hymn Book Supplement*)	46,* 49, 5
,,	USPG	2
Arlott, J.	Author	3
Bayly, A. F.	Oxford University Press	60, 64, 78,* 82, 99
Bell, G. K. A.	Oxford University Press (from *Enlarged Songs of Praise*)	12
Bowie, W. Russell	Abingdon Press, Nashville, USA (from *Lift up your hearts*)	5
,,	Harper & Brothers, New York (from *Hymns of the Kingdom of God*)	7
Bridge, B. E.	Free Church Choir Union	9
Briggs, G. W.	Oxford University Press (from *Enlarged Songs of Praise*)	13, 1
,,	Oxford University Press	50, 69, 8
Brooks, R. T.	Agape, Carol Stream, Il 60187, USA	9
Burns, E. J.	Author	9
Caird, G. B.	The Exors. of the late G. B. Caird	68
,,	Independent Press, Ltd.	
Carter, S.	Essex Music, Ltd.	6
,,	Galliard, Ltd. (from *Songs of Sydney Carter in the Present Tense, Book 3*)	21, 100
,,	Galliard, Ltd. (from *Songs of Sydney Carter in the Present Tense, Book 2*)	42
von Christierson, F.	The Hymn Society of America	44
Clare, J.	E. Blunden	
Cross, S.	Author	2
Crum, J. M. C.	Mrs Mary Wright	3
Dearmer, G.	Author	
Dearmer, P.	Oxford University Press (from *Enlarged Songs of Praise*)	8, 5
,,	Oxford University Press (from *The English Hymnal*)	4
,, and Humphreys, C. W. (trans)	Oxford University Press (from *The English Hymnal*)	8
Dudley-Smith, T.	Author	8
Edge, D.	Author	6
Fosdick, H. E.	The Exors of the late H. L. Fosdick	34

TUNES

COMPOSER	PERMISSION GRANTED BY	NO. OF HYMN
Buck, Sir Percy . . .	Oxford University Press	55
Carter, S.	Essex Music, Ltd, ...	67
,, ...	Galliard, Ltd. (from *Songs of Sydney Carter in the Present Tense, Book 3*)	21, 100
,, ...	Galliard, Ltd. (from *Songs of Sydney Carter in the Present Tense, Book 2*)	42
Cutts, P.	Oxford University Press	7, 16, 53
Douglas, W. (har.) . . .	The Church Pension Fund, New York . . .	76(*ii*)
Evans, D. (har.) . . .	Oxford University Press (from *The Revised Church Hymnary*)	50, 71
Gibbs, A.	J. Curwen & Sons, Ltd.	63(*i*)
Greatorex, W.	Oxford University Press	89
Howells, H.	Novello & Co., Ltd.	3, 76(*i*)
Ireland, J.	John Ireland Trust	30
McKie, Sir William (har.)	McKie, Sir William	93
Murrill, H.	Mrs Frith	35
Nicholson, Sir Sydney (arr.)	Royal School of Church Music	44
Routley, E.	Oxford University Press	99
,, (har.) . . .	Oxford University Press	10, 62
Shaw, G. (har.) . . .	Oxford University Press (from *Enlarged Songs of Praise*)	5
Slater, G.	Oxford University Press (from *Songs of Praise for Boys and Girls*)	27
Stanton, W. K.	Oxford University Press (from *The BBC Hymn Book*)	38
Taylor, C. V.	Oxford University Press . . . 33, 59, 66(*i*)	
,, ...	Oxford University Press (from *The BBC Hymn Book*)	23, 61
Thiman, E.	Independent Press, Ltd.	11
Vaughan Williams, R. (har.)	Oxford University Press (from *The English Hymnal*) . . . . . 6, 25, 45, 52, 66(*ii*), 80	
,,	Oxford University Press (from *Enlarged Songs of Praise*)	60
,,	Stainer & Bell, Ltd.	77
Watson, S.	Composer	56
Westbrook, F. B. . . .	Oxford University Press	81
Wood, Thomas	Oxford University Press (from *Enlarged Songs of Praise*)	78

The following copyright hymns belong to *Hymns Ancient and Modern Limited:* 38, 81.

Also the following copyright tunes or arrangements: 1, 8, 9, 15(*i*), 18, 24, 40, 54, 57, 65, 70, 75, 82.

The organ arrangements for tunes 21, 42, 49, 58, 67 and 100 are by John Birch.

COPYRIGHT

GRANTS

An asterisk placed before the number of a verse indicates that the verse may be omitted, if so desired. An asterisk placed after an author's name denotes some alteration of the original words.

The hymns are arranged alphabetically.

1 Tyrol D.C.M.   Tyrolean Melody

Lively

The Man for Others

A Man there lived in Galilee
  unlike all men before,
For he alone from first to last
  our flesh unsullied wore;
A perfect life of perfect deeds
  once to the world was shown,
That all mankind might mark his steps
  and in them plant their own.

2

A Man there died on Calvary
  above all others brave;
His fellow-men he saved and blessed,
  himself he scorned to save.
No thought can gauge the weight of woe
  on him, the sinless, laid;
We only know that with his blood
  our ransom price was paid.

3

A Man there reigns in glory now,
  divine, yet human still;
That human which is all divine
  death sought in vain to kill.
All power is his; supreme he rules
  the realms of time and space;
Yet still our human cares and needs
  find in his heart a place.

S. C. LOWRY* (1855–1932)

2 Surrey   8 8.8 8.8 8.   Henry Carey (c. 1690–1743)

The Stranger

A stranger once did bless the earth
    who never caused a heart to mourn,
Whose very voice gave sorrow mirth;
    and how did earth his worth return?
It spurned him from its lowliest lot:
The meanest station owned him not.

2

An outcast thrown in sorrow's way,
    a fugitive that knew no sin,
Yet in lone places forced to stray;
    men would not take the stranger in.
Yet peace, though much himself he mourned,
Was all to others he returned.

3

His presence was a peace to all,
    he bade the sorrowful rejoice.
Pain turned to pleasure at his call,
    health lived and issued from his voice;
He healed the sick, and sent abroad
The dumb rejoicing in the Lord.

4

The blind met daylight in his eye,
    the joys of everlasting day;
The sick found health in his reply,
    the cripple threw his crutch away.
Yet he with troubles did remain,
And suffered poverty and pain.

5

It was for sin he suffered all
    to set the world-imprisoned free,
To cheer the weary when they call;
    and who could such a stranger be?
The God, who hears each human cry,
And came, a Saviour, from on high.

JOHN CLARE* (1793–1864)

3 Michael 8 7.8 7.3 3 7   Herbert Howells (1892–1983)

God our Hope

All my hope on God is founded;
  he doth still my trust renew.
Me through change and chance he guideth,
  only good and only true.
      God unknown,
      He alone
  Calls my heart to be his own.

2

Pride of man and earthly glory,
  sword and crown betray his trust;
What with care and toil he buildeth,
  tower and temple, fall to dust.
      But God's power,
      Hour by hour,
  Is my temple and my tower.

3

God's great goodness aye endureth,
  deep his wisdom, passing thought:
Splendour, light, and life attend him,
  beauty springeth out of naught.
      Evermore
      From his store
  New-born worlds rise and adore.

*4

Daily doth th' Almighty Giver
  bounteous gifts on us bestow;
His desire our soul delighteth,
  pleasure leads us where we go.
      Love doth stand
      At his hand;
  Joy doth wait on his command.

5

Still from man to God eternal
  sacrifice of praise be done,
High above all praises praising
  for the gift of Christ his Son.
      Christ doth call
      One and all:
  Ye who follow shall not fall.

ROBERT BRIDGES (1844–1930)
based on the German of J. Neander (1650–80)

C. V. Stanford (1852–1924)

Al - - le-lu - ia   Al - - le-lu - ia

Humility and Glory

All praise to thee, for thou, O King divine,
Didst yield the glory that of right was thine,
That in our darkened hearts thy grace might shine:
Alleluia.

2

Thou cam'st to us in lowliness of thought;
By thee the outcast and the poor were sought,
And by thy death was God's salvation wrought:
Alleluia.

3

Let this mind be in us which was in thee,
Who wast a servant that we might be free,
Humbling thyself to death on Calvary:
Alleluia.

4

Wherefore, by God's eternal purpose, thou
Art high exalted o'er all creatures now,
And giv'n the name to which all knees shall bow:
Alleluia.

5

Let ev'ry tongue confess with one accord
In heav'n and earth that Jesus Christ is Lord;
And God the Father be by all adored:
Alleluia.

F. BLAND TUCKER (1895–1984)
based on Philippians 2, 5–11

The Claims of Love

Almighty Father, who for us thy Son didst give,
That men and nations through his precious death
    might live,
In mercy guard us, lest by sloth and selfish
    pride
We cause to stumble those for whom the
    Saviour died.

2

We are thy stewards; thine our talents,
    wisdom, skill;
Our only glory that we may thy trust fulfil;
That we thy pleasure in our neighbours'
    good pursue,
If thou but workest in us both to will and do.

3

On just and unjust thou thy care dost freely
    shower;
Make us, thy children, free from greed and
    lust for power,
Lest human justice, yoked with man's
    unequal laws,
Oppress the needy and neglect the humble
    cause.

4

Let not our worship blind us to the claims of
    love,
But let thy manna lead us to the feast above,
To seek the country which by faith we now
    possess,
Where Christ, our treasure, reigns in peace
    and righteousness.

GEORGE B. CAIRD (1917–84)

The Healing Christ

1

And didst thou travel light, dear Lord,
  was thine so smooth a road
That thou upon thy shoulders broad
  could hoist our heavy load?
Too frail each other's woes to bear
  without thy help are we;
Can we each other's burdens share
  if we not burden thee?

2

O wonder of the world withstood!
  That night of prayer and doom
Was not the sunset red with blood,
  the dawn pale as a tomb?
In agony and bloody sweat,
  in tears of love undried,
O undespairing Lord, and yet⏝
  with man identified.

3

As in dark drops the pitting rain⏝
  falls on a dusty street,
So tears shall fall and fall again
  to wash thy wounded feet.
But thy quick hands to heal are strong,
  O love, thy patients we,
Who sing with joy the pilgrims' song
  and walk, dear Lord, with thee.

GEOFFREY DEARMER (b. 1893)

Peter Cutts (b. 1937)

A and B may be sung by contrasted groups of voices

Belonging

1

As the bridegroom to his chosen,
　as the king unto his realm,
As the keep unto the castle,
　as the pilot to the helm,
So, Lord, art thou to me.

2

As the fountain in the garden,
　as the candle in the dark,
As the treasure in the coffer,
　as the manna in the ark,
So, Lord, art thou to me.

3

As the music at the banquet,
　as the stamp unto the seal,
As the medicine to the fainting,
　as the wine-cup at the meal,
So, Lord, art thou to me.

4

As the ruby in the setting,
　as the honey in the comb,
As the light within the lantern,
　as the father in the home,
So, Lord, art thou to me.

5

As the sunshine in the heavens,
　as the image in the glass,
As the fruit unto the fig-tree,
　as the dew unto the grass,
So, Lord, art thou to me.

Par. from (?) JOHN TAULER (1300–61)
by Emma Frances Bevan (1827–1909)

8 Diva servatrix 11 11 11.5.   Melody from *Bayeux Antiphoner, 1739*

The tune is sung twice for each verse, with first and second endings

The Love Feast

Choir or Solo   As the disciples, when thy Son had left them,
          met in a love-feast, joyfully conversing,
All the stored memory of the Lord's last supper
          fondly rehearsing;

All   So may we here, who gather now in friendship,
          seek for the spirit of those earlier Churches,
Welcoming him who stands and for an entrance
          patiently searches.

2

Choir or Solo   As, when their converse closed and supper ended,
          taking the bread and wine they made thanksgiving,
Breaking and blessing, thus to have communion
          with Christ the living;

All   So may we here, a company of brothers,
          make this our love-feast and commemoration,
That in his Spirit we may have more worthy
          participation.

3

Choir or Solo   And as they prayed and sang to thee rejoicing,
          ere in the night-fall they embraced and parted,
In their hearts singing as they journeyed homeward,
          brave and true-hearted;

All   So may we here, like corn that once was scattered
          over the hill-side, now one bread united,
Led by the Spirit, do thy work rejoicing,
          lamps filled and lighted.

PERCY DEARMER (1867–1936)

9 Grenoble (Deus tuorum militum) L.M.

Melody from *Grenoble Antiphoner, 1753*

The New Life

1

Awake, awake: fling off the night!
For God has sent his glorious light;
   And we who live in Christ's new day
   must works of darkness put away.

2

Awake and rise, like men renewed,
men with the Spirit's power endued.
   The light of life in us must glow,
   and fruits of truth and goodness show.

3

Let in the light; all sin expose
to Christ, whose life no darkness knows.
   Before his cross for guidance kneel;
   his light will judge and, judging, heal.

4

Awake, and rise up from the dead,
and Christ his light on you will shed.
   Its power will wrong desires destroy,
   and your whole nature fill with joy.

5

Then sing for joy, and use each day;
give thanks for everything alway.
   Lift up your hearts; with one accord
   praise God through Jesus Christ our Lord.

J. R. PEACEY (1896–1971)
based on Ephesians 5, 6–20
(possibly a hymn for baptism)

First and Last

Be thou my vision, O Lord of my heart,
Be all else but naught to me, save that thou art;
   Be thou my best thought in the day and the night,
   Both waking and sleeping, thy presence my light.

2

Be thou my wisdom, be thou my true word,
Be thou ever with me, and I with thee, Lord;
   Be thou my great Father, and I thy true son;
   Be thou in me dwelling, and I with thee one.

3

Be thou my breastplate, my sword for the fight;
Be thou my whole armour, be thou my true might;
   Be thou my soul's shelter, be thou my strong tower:
   O raise thou me heavenward, great Power of my power.

4

Riches I heed not, nor man's empty praise:
Be thou mine inheritance now and always;
   Be thou and thou only the first in my heart:
   O Sovereign of heaven, my treasure thou art.

5

High King of heaven, thou heaven's bright Sun,
O grant me its joys after vict'ry is won;
   Great Heart of my own heart, whatever befall,
   Still be thou my vision, O Ruler of all.

                           Irish, c. 8th century
                           tr. Mary Byrne (1880–1931)
                versified, Eleanor Hull (1860–1935)

Christ for the World

Christ for the world we sing!
The world to Christ we bring
  with fervent prayer;
The wayward and the lost,
By restless passions tossed,
Redeemed at countless cost
  from dark despair.

2

Christ for the world we sing!
The world to Christ we bring
  with one accord;
With us the work to share,
With us reproach to dare,
With us the cross to bear,
  for Christ our Lord.

3

Christ for the world we sing!
The world to Christ we bring
  with joyful song;
The new-born souls, whose days,
Reclaimed from error's ways,
Inspired with hope and praise,
  to Christ belong.

SAMUEL WOLCOTT (1813–86)

12 Gelobt sei Gott 8 8 8. with Alleluias
(Vulpius)

Melody from M. Vulpius
Gesangbuch, 1609

Al - le - lu - ia. _____ Al - le - lu - ia. _____ Al - le - lu - ia.

Christ the King

1

Christ is the King! O friends rejoice;
Brothers and sisters, with one voice
Make all men know he is your choice.
Alleluia.

2

O magnify the Lord, and raise
Anthems of joy and holy praise
For Christ's brave saints of ancient days.
Alleluia.

3

They with a faith for ever new
Followed the King, and round him drew
Thousands of faithful men and true.
Alleluia.

4

O Christian women, Christian men,
All the world over, seek again
The Way disciples followed then.
Alleluia.

5

Christ through all ages is the same:
Place the same hope in his great name,
With the same faith his word proclaim.
Alleluia.

6

Let Love's unconquerable might
Your scattered companies unite
In service to the Lord of light.
Alleluia.

7

So shall God's will on earth be done,
New lamps be lit, new tasks begun,
And the whole Church at last be one.
Alleluia.

G. K. A. BELL* (1883–1958)

13 Darmstadt 6 7.6 7.6 6.6 6.

Melody by A. Fritsch (1679)
Adapted by J. S. Bach (1685–1750)

The Hope of the World

1

Christ is the world's true light,
  its captain of salvation,
The daystar clear and bright
  of every man and nation;
New life, new hope awakes,
  where'er men own his sway:
Freedom her bondage breaks,
  and night is turned to day.

2

In Christ all races meet,
  their ancient feuds forgetting,
The whole round world complete,
  from sunrise to its setting:
When Christ is throned as Lord,
  men shall forsake their fear,
To ploughshare beat the sword,
  to pruning-hook the spear.

3

One Lord, in one great name
  unite us all who own thee;
Cast out our pride and shame
  that hinder to enthrone thee;
The world has waited long,
  has travailed long in pain;
To heal its ancient wrong,
  come, Prince of Peace, and reign!

G. W. BRIGGS (1875–1959)

The Hope of Glory

Christ, who knows all his sheep,
Will all in safety keep:
He will not lose one soul,
   nor ever fail us:
Nor we the promised goal,
   whate'er assail us.

2

We know our God is just;
To him we wholly trust
All that we have and claim,
   and all we hope for:
All's sure and seen to him,
   which here we grope for.

3

Fear not the world of light,
Though out of mortal sight;
There shall we know God more,
   where all is holy:
There is no grief or care,
   no sin or folly.

4

O blessèd company,
Where all in harmony
God's joyous praises sing,
   in love unceasing;
And all obey their King,
   with perfect pleasing.

Adapted from RICHARD BAXTER (1615–91)

15

Quedgeley 7 6. 7 6.   John Dykes Bower (1905–81)

Melling 7 6. 7 6.   John Fawcett (1789–1867)

The Gospel

Come, Lord, to our souls come down,
    through the Gospel speaking;
Let your words, your cross and crown,
    lighten all our seeking.

2

Drive out darkness from the heart,
    banish pride and blindness;
Plant in every inward part
    truthfulness and kindness.

3

Eyes be open, spirits stirred,
    minds new truth receiving;
Make us, Lord, by your own Word,
    more and more believing.

H. C. A. GAUNT (1902–83)

Alternative Tune: *Adoro te* (A.M.R. 385; E.H. 331; S.P. 279)

The Breaking of Bread

Come, risen Lord, and deign to be our guest;
   nay, let us be thy guests; the feast is thine;
Thyself at thine own board make manifest,
   in thine own sacrament of bread and wine.

2

We meet, as in that upper room they met;
   thou at the table, blessing, yet dost stand:
'This is my body': so thou givest yet:
   faith still receives the cup as from thy hand.

3

One body we, one body who partake,
   one church united in communion blest;
One name we bear, one bread of life we break,
   with all thy saints on earth and saints at rest.

4

One with each other, Lord, for one in thee,
   who art one Saviour and one living Head;
Then open thou our eyes, that we may see;
   be known to us in breaking of the bread.

G. W. BRIGGS (1875–1959)

James Leach (1762–98)

Alternative Tune: *Narenza* (A.M.R. 229; E.H. 518; C.P. 493)

Daily Work

Come, workers for the Lord
And lift up heart and hand;
Praise God, all skill at bench and board,
Praise, all that brain has planned.

2

When Christ to manhood came
A craftsman was he made
And served his glad apprentice time
Bound to the joiner's trade.

3

When Christ on Calvary
Drank down his cruel draught,
The men who nailed him to the tree
Were men of his own craft.

4

So, God, our labour take,
From spite and greed set free;
May nothing that we do or make
Bring ill to man or thee.

5

All workers for the Lord,
Come sing with voice and heart;
In strength of hands be God adored
And praised in power of art.

NORMAN NICHOLSON (b. 1914)

Alternative Tune: *Breslau*, 64 (E.H. 484; S.P. 132; C.P. 378)

The Unknown God

Creator of the earth and skies,
    to whom all truth and power belong,
Grant us your truth to make us wise;
    grant us your power to make us strong.

2

We have not known you: to the skies
    our monuments of folly soar,
And all our self-wrought miseries
    have made us trust ourselves the more.

3

We have not loved you: far and wide
    the wreckage of our hatred spreads,
And evils wrought by human pride
    recoil on unrepentant heads.

4

We long to end this worldwide strife:
    how shall we follow in your way?
Speak to mankind your words of life,
    until our darkness turns to day.

DONALD WYNN HUGHES* (1911–67)

19 Song 24 10 10. 10 10. 10 10. Orlando Gibbons (1583–1625)

Alternative Tune: *Song 1, 20* (E.H. 302; S.P. 296; C.P. 554)

Bread and Wine

He took

Dear Lord, to you again our gifts we bring,
  this bread our toil, this wine our ecstasy,
    poor and imperfect though they both must be;
Yet you will take a heart-free offering.
Yours is the bounty, ours the unfettered will
To make or mar, to fashion good or ill.

He blessed   2

Yes, you will take and bless, and grace impart
  to make again what once your goodness gave,
    what we half crave, and half refuse to have,
A sturdier will, a more repentant heart.
You have on earth no hands, no hearts but ours;
Bless them as yours, ourselves, our will, our powers.

He broke   3

Break bread, O Lord, break down our wayward wills,
  break down our prized possessions, break them down;
    let them be freely given as your own
To all who need our gifts, to heal their ills.
Break this, the bread we bring, that all may share
In your one living body, everywhere.

He gave   4

Our lips receive your wine, our hands your bread;
  you give us back the selves we offered you,
    won by the Cross, by Calvary made new,
A heart enriched, a life raised from the dead.
Grant us to take and guard your treasure well,
That we in you, and you in us may dwell.

                              H. C. A. GAUNT (1902–83)

Unity in the Spirit

Eternal Ruler of the ceaseless round
  of circling planets singing on their way;
Guide of the nations from the night profound
  into the glory of the perfect day;
Rule in our hearts, that we may ever be
Guided and strengthened and upheld by thee.

2

We are of thee, the children of thy love,
  the brothers of thy well-belovèd Son;
Descend, O Holy Spirit, like a dove,
  into our hearts, that we may be as one:
As one with thee, to whom we ever tend;
As one with him, our Brother and our Friend.

3

We would be one in hatred of all wrong,
  one in our love of all things sweet and fair,
One with the joy that breaketh into song,
  one with the grief that trembles into prayer,
One in the power that makes thy children free
To follow truth, and thus to follow thee.

4

O clothe us with thy heavenly armour, Lord,
  thy trusty shield, thy sword of love divine;
Our inspiration be thy constant word;
  we ask no victories that are not thine:
Give or withhold, let pain or pleasure be;
Enough to know that we are serving thee.

J. W. CHADWICK (1840–1904)

21 Every Star   Sydney Carter (b. 1915)

God a - bove, Man be - low, Ho - ly is the name I know.

A Carol of the Universe

1

Solo (or a few voices)
Every star shall sing a carol;
  every creature, high or low,
Come and praise the King of Heaven,
  by whatever name you know.

All
God above, Man below,
  Holy is the name I know.

2

When the King of all creation
  had a cradle on the earth,
Holy was the human body,
  holy was the human birth:

3

Who can tell what other cradle
  high above the milky way
Still may rock the King of Heaven
  on another Christmas Day?

4

Who can count how many crosses
  still to come or long ago
Crucify the King of Heaven?
  holy is the name I know:

5

Who can tell what other body
  he will hallow for his own?
I will praise the Son of Mary,
  brother of my blood and bone:

6

Every star and every planet,
  every creature high and low,
Come and praise the King of Heaven,
  by whatever name you know:

SYDNEY CARTER (b. 1915)

22(i) Was lebet 12 10. 12 10. *Rheinhardt MS. (Üttingen, 1754)*

The two parts of this hymn may be used separately.
If both parts are combined, verses 2, 4, 6 may be sung by soloist or choir.

Alive for God

PART 1

Father all-pow-erful, thine is the kingdom,
　thine is the pow-er, the glory of love;
Gently thou carest for each of thy children,
　lovingly sending thy Son from above.

3

Crucified Jesus, thou bearest our wickedness,
　now thou art risen that all men may live;
Mighty Redeemer, despite our unworthiness,
　thou in thy mercy our sins dost forgive.

5

Comforter, Spirit, thou camest at Pentecost,
　pouring thy grace on thy Church here below;
Still thou dost feed us by prayer and by sacrament,
　till all creation thy glory shall know.

7

Holiest Trinity, perfect in Unity,
　bind in thy love every nation and race:
May we adore thee for time and eternity,
　Father, Redeemer, and Spirit of grace.

PATRICK APPLEFORD (b. 1924)

The two parts of this hymn may be used separately.
If both parts are combined, verses 2, 4, 6 may be sung by soloist or choir.

Alive for God

PART 2

2

Father all-loving, thou rulest in majesty,
  judgment is thine, and condemneth our pride;
Stir up our rulers and peoples to penitence,
  sorrow for sins that for vengeance have cried.

4

Blessèd Lord Jesus, thou camest in poverty,
  sharing a stable with beasts at thy birth;
Stir us to work for thy justice and charity,
  truly to care for the poor upon earth.

6

Come, Holy Spirit, create in us holiness,
  lift up our lives to thy standard of right;
Stir every will to new ventures of faithfulness,
  flood the whole Church with thy glorious light.

7

Holiest Trinity, perfect in Unity,
  bind in thy love every nation and race:
May we adore thee for time and eternity,
  Father, Redeemer, and Spirit of grace.

PATRICK APPLEFORD (b. 1924)

23 Abbot's Leigh 8 7.8 7.D.

Cyril Taylor (b. 1907)

Renewal

Father, Lord of all Creation,
    Ground of Being, Life and Love;
Height and depth beyond description
    only life in you can prove:
You are mortal life's dependence:
    thought, speech, sight are ours by grace;
Yours is every hour's existence,
    sovereign Lord of time and space.

2

Jesus Christ, the Man for Others,
    we, your people, make our prayer:
Give us grace to love as brothers
    all whose burdens we can share.
Where your name binds us together
    you, Lord Christ, will surely be;
Where no selfishness can sever
    there your love may all men see.

3

Holy Spirit, rushing, burning
    wind and flame of Pentecost,
Fire our hearts afresh with yearning
    to regain what we have lost.
May your love unite our action,
    nevermore to speak alone:
God, in us abolish faction,
    God, through us your love make known

STEWART CROSS (b. 19

The Living Bread

Father, we thank thee who hast planted
    thy holy name within our hearts.
Knowledge and faith and life immortal
    Jesus thy Son to us imparts.

2

Thou, Lord, didst make all for thy pleasure,
    didst give man food for all his days,
Giving in Christ the bread eternal;
    thine is the power, be thine the praise.

3

Watch o'er thy Church, O Lord, in mercy,
    save it from evil, guard it still,
Perfect it in thy love, unite it,
    cleansed and conformed unto thy will.

4

As grain, once scattered on the hillsides,
    was in this broken bread made one,
So from all lands thy Church be gathered
    into thy kingdom by thy Son.

From the *Didache*,
(1st or 2nd century)
tr. F. BLAND TUCKER (1895–1984)

Into the World

Father, who in Jesus found us,
God, whose love is all around us,
who to freedom new unbound us,
    keep our hearts with joy aflame.

2

For the sacramental breaking,
for the honour of partaking,
for your life our lives remaking,
    young and old, we praise your name.

3

From the service of this table
lead us to a life more stable;
for our witness make us able;
    blessing on our work we claim.

4

Through our calling closely knitted,
daily to your praise committed,
for a life of service fitted,
    let us now your love proclaim.

FRED KAAN (b. 1929)

Fellowship in the Holy Spirit

Filled with the Spirit's power, with one accord
the infant Church confessed its risen Lord.
    O Holy Spirit, in the Church to-day
    no less your power of fellowship display.

2

Now with the mind of Christ set us on fire,
that unity may be our great desire.
    Give joy and peace; give faith to hear your call,
    and readiness in each to work for all.

3

Widen our love, good Spirit, to embrace
in your strong care the men of every race.
    Like wind and fire with life among us move,
    till we are known as Christ's, and Christians prove.

J. R. Peacey (1896–1971)

Mother of the Lord

1

For Mary, Mother of our Lord,
  God's holy name be praised,
Who first the Son of God adored,
  as on her child she gazed.

2

Brave, holy Virgin, she believed,
  though hard the task assigned,
And by the Holy Ghost conceived
  the Saviour of mankind.

*3

God's handmaid, she at once obeyed,
  by her 'Thy will be done';
The second Eve love's answer made
  which our redemption won.

*4

The busy world had got no space
  or time for God on earth;
A cattle manger was the place
  where Mary gave him birth.

5

She gave her body as God's shrine,
  her heart to piercing pain;
She knew the cost of love divine,
  when Jesus Christ was slain.

6

Dear Mary, from your lowliness
  and home in Galilee
There comes a joy and holiness
  to every family.

7

Hail, Mary, you are full of grace,
  above all women blest;
And blest your Son, whom your embrace
  in birth and death confessed.

J. R. Peacey (1896–1971)

28 Alleluia, dulce carmen   8 7.8 7.8 7.

Essay on the Church Plain Chant, 1782

Human Rights

For the healing of the nations,
  Lord, we pray with one accord;
For a just and equal sharing
  of the things that earth affords.
To a life of love in action
  help us rise and pledge our word.

2

Lead us, Father, into freedom,
  from despair your world release;
That, redeemed from war and hatred,
  men may come and go in peace.
Show us how through care and goodness
  fear will die and hope increase.

3

All that kills abundant living,
  let it from the earth be banned;
Pride of status, race or schooling,
  dogmas keeping man from man.
In our common quest for justice
  may we hallow life's brief span.

4

You, creator-God, have written
  your great name on all mankind;
For our growing in your likeness
  bring the life of Christ to mind;
That by our response and service
  earth its destiny may find.

FRED KAAN (b. 1929)

Melody from *A Book of Psalmody*
by James Green (c. 1690–1750)

Alternative Tune: *St. Bernard* (A.M.R. 104; E.H. 71; S.P. 537; C.P. 346)

The Unforgiving Heart

'Forgive our sins as we forgive'
  you taught us, Lord, to pray;
But you alone can grant us grace
  to live the words we say.

2

How can your pardon reach and bless
  the unforgiving heart
That broods on wrongs, and will not let
  old bitterness depart?

3

In blazing light your Cross reveals
  the truth we dimly knew,
How small the debts men owe to us,
  how great our debt to you.

4

Lord, cleanse the depths within our souls,
  and bid resentment cease;
Then, reconciled to God and man,
  our lives will spread your peace.

ROSAMOND E. HERKLOTS (b. 1905)

All Saints

Glory to thee, O God,
  for all thy saints in light,
who nobly strove and conquered in the well-fought fight.
  Their praises sing,
  who life outpoured
by fire and sword for Christ their King.

2

Thanks be to thee, O Lord,
  for saints thy Spirit stirred
in humble paths to live thy life and speak thy word.
  Unnumbered they,
  whose candles shine
to lead our footsteps after thine.

3

Lord God of truth and love,
  'thy kingdom come', we pray;
give us thy grace to know thy truth and walk thy way:
  That here on earth
  thy will be done,
till saints in earth and heaven are one.

H. C. A. GAUNT (1902–83)

Light, Love, and Life

God is Light,
away with blindness and unkindness;
all that's bright⌣
is shining with his light.
Turn to him; if anything would dim⌣
the light of happiness and praise
   and thankfulness to him.

2

God is Love,
and he rejoices in our voices,
God is Love,
around us and above.
Ask we him to fill our hearts with love,
to fill our thankful hearts with love⌣
   and gladness to the brim.

3

God is Life,
his everlasting Son is giving⌣
happy life
to those who trust in him.
Praises be, O risen Christ, to thee;
for thou hast set us free to live⌣
   in thankfulness to thee.

J. M. C. CRUM (1872–1958)

32 Alleluia 8 7. 8 7. D.   S. S. Wesley (1810–76)

Alternative Tune: *Hyfrydol* (A.M.R. 260; E.H. 301; S.P. 260; C.P. 179)

God is Love

1

God is Love: let heav'n adore him;
  God is Love: let earth rejoice;
Let creation sing before him,
  and exalt him with one voice.
He who laid the earth's foundation,
  he who spread the heav'ns above,
He who breathes through all creation,
  he is Love, eternal Love.

2

God is Love: and he enfoldeth
  all the world in one embrace;
With unfailing grasp he holdeth
  every child of every race.
And when human hearts are breaking
  under sorrow's iron rod,
Then they find that selfsame aching
  deep within the heart of God.

3

God is Love: and though with blindness
  sin afflicts the souls of men,
God's eternal loving-kindness
  holds and guides them even then.
Sin and death and hell shall never
  o'er us final triumph gain;
God is Love, so Love for ever
  o'er the universe must reign.

TIMOTHY REES* (1874–1939)

33 Minterne 7 7.7 7.7 7.

Cyril Taylor (b. 1907)

The Earth is the Lord's

God of concrete, God of steel,
God of piston and of wheel,
God of pylon, God of steam,
God of girder and of beam,
God of atom, God of mine,
All the world of power is thine.

2

Lord of cable, Lord of rail,
Lord of motorway and mail,
Lord of rocket, Lord of flight,
Lord of soaring satellite,
Lord of lightning's livid line,
All the world of speed is thine.

3

Lord of science, Lord of art,
God of map and graph and chart,
Lord of physics and research,
Word of Bible, Faith of Church,
Lord of sequence and design,
All the world of truth is thine.

4

God whose glory fills the earth,
Gave the universe its birth,
Loosed the Christ with Easter's might,
Saves the world from evil's blight,
Claims mankind by grace divine,
All the world of love is thine.

RICHARD G. JONES (b. 1926)

Henry Smart (1813–79)

Faith for Living

God of grace and God of glory,
   on thy people pour thy power;
Now fulfil thy Church's story;
   bring her bud to glorious flower.
Grant us wisdom, grant us courage,
   for the facing of this hour.

2

Lo, the hosts of evil round us
   scorn thy Christ, assail his ways;
From the fears that long have bound us
   free our hearts to faith and praise.
Grant us wisdom, grant us courage,
   for the living of these days.

3

Cure thy children's warring madness,
   bend our pride to thy control;
Shame our wanton selfish gladness,
   rich in goods and poor in soul.
Grant us wisdom, grant us courage,
   lest we miss thy kingdom's goal.

4

Set our feet on lofty places,
   gird our lives that they may be
Armoured with all Christlike graces
   in the fight to set men free.
Grant us wisdom, grant us courage,
   that we fail not man nor thee.

H. E. FOSDICK* (1878–1969)

35 Carolyn 8 5.8 5.8 5.8 8.8 5. Herbert Murrill (1909–52)

Hallowed be thy Name

God of love and truth and beauty,
   hallowed be thy name;
Fount of order, law, and duty,
   hallowed be thy name.
As in heaven thy hosts adore thee,
And their faces veil before thee,
So on earth, Lord, we implore thee,
   hallowed be thy name.

2

Lord, remove our guilty blindness,
   hallowed be thy name;
Show thy heart of loving kindness,
   hallowed be thy name.
By our heart's deep-felt contrition,
By our mind's enlightened vision,
By our will's complete submission,
   hallowed be thy name.

3

In our worship, Lord most holy,
   hallowed be thy name;
In our work, however lowly,
   hallowed be thy name.
In each heart's imagination,
In the Church's adoration,
In the conscience of the nation,
   hallowed be thy name.

TIMOTHY REES (1874–1939)

36 Quedlinburg 10 10. 10 10.

From a Chorale by J. C. Kittel
(1732–1809)

Adam

God who created this Eden of earth
Giving to Adam and Eve their fresh birth,
What have we done with that wonderful tree?
    Lord, forgive Adam,
    For Adam is me.

2

Adam ambitious desires to be wise,
Casts out obedience, then lusts with his eyes;
Grasps his sweet fruit, 'As God I shall be'.
    Lord, forgive Adam,
    For Adam is me.

3

Thirst after pow'r is this sin of my shame,
Pride's ruthless thrust after status and fame,
Turning and stealing and cowering from thee.
    Lord, forgive Adam,
    For Adam is me.

4

Cursed is the earth through this cancerous crime,
Symbol of man through all passage of time,
Put it all right, Lord; let Adam be free;
    Do it for Adam,
    For Adam is me.

5

Glory to God! what is this that I see?
Man made anew, second Adam is he,
Bleeding his love on another fine tree;
    Dies second Adam,
    Young Adam, for me.

6

Rises that Adam the master of death,
Pours out his Spirit in holy new breath
Sheer liberation! With him I am free!
    Lives second Adam
    In mercy in me.

RICHARD G. JONES (b. 1926)

37 Gott will's machen 8 7. 8 7. J. L. Steiner (1688–1761)

God's Farm

God, whose farm is all creation,
 take the gratitude we give;
Take the finest of our harvest,
 crops we grow that men may live.

2

Take our ploughing, seeding, reaping,
 hopes and fears of sun and rain,
All our thinking, planning, waiting,
 ripened in this fruit and grain.

3

All our labour, all our watching,
 all our calendar of care,
In these crops of your creation,
 take, O God: they are our prayer.

JOHN ARLOTT (b. 1914)

38 Hambleden   8 9.8 9.D.   W. K. Stanton (1891–1978)

Offertory

Good is our God who made this place
    whereon our race in plenty liveth.
Great is the praise to him we owe,
    that we may show 'tis he that giveth.
Then let who would for daily food
    give thanks to God who life preserveth;
Offer this board to our good Lord,
    and him applaud who praise deserveth.

2

Praise him again whose sovereign will
    grants us the skill of daily labour;
Whose blessèd Son to our great good
    fashioned his wood to serve his neighbour.
Shall we who sing not also bring⌣
    of this world's wages to the Table?
Giving again of what we gain,
    to make it plain God doth enable.

3

So let us our Creator praise,
    who all our days our life sustaineth;
Offer our work, renew our vow,
    adore him now who rightly reigneth;
That we who break this bread, and take⌣
    this cup of Christ to our enjoyment,
May so believe, so well receive,
    never to leave our Lord's employment.

J. K. Gregory (b. 1929)

Trusting God

Have faith in God, my heart,
  trust and be unafraid;
God will fulfil in every part
  each promise he has made.

2

Have faith in God, my mind,
  though oft thy light burns low;
God's mercy holds a wiser plan
  than thou canst fully know.

3

Have faith in God, my soul,
  his Cross for ever stands;
And neither life nor death can pluck
  his children from his hands.

4

Lord Jesus, make me whole;
  grant me no resting place,
Until I rest, heart, mind, and soul,
  the captive of thy grace.

B. A. REES (1911–84)

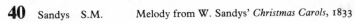 Melody from W. Sandys' *Christmas Carols*, 1833

Living the Faith

Help us, O Lord, to learn
  the truths thy Word imparts:
To study that thy laws may be
  inscribed upon our hearts.

2

Help us, O Lord, to live
  the faith which we proclaim,
That all our thoughts and words and deeds
  may glorify thy name.

3

Help us, O Lord, to teach
  the beauty of thy ways,
That yearning souls may find the Christ,
  and sing aloud his praise.

WILLIAM WATKINS REID (b. 1923)

Charity

Help us to help each other, Lord,
  each other's cross to bear;
Let each his friendly aid afford,
  and feel his brother's care.

2

Up into thee, our living head,
  let us in all things grow,
And by thy sacrifice be led
  the fruits of love to show.

3

Drawn by the magnet of thy love
  let all our hearts agree;
And ever towards each other move,
  and ever move towards thee.

4

This is the bond of perfectness,
  thy spotless charity.
O let us still, we pray, possess
  the mind that was in thee.

Cento from Charles Wesley*
(1707–88)

Adapted by Sydney Carter (b. 1915)

(Two bars organ introduction)

Solo Lively and rhythmic

All in Unison

Dance, then, wher-ev-er you may be;

I am the Lord of the Dance, said he, And I'll lead you all, wher-

ev-er you may be, And I'll lead you all in the dance, said he.

Melody of last verse

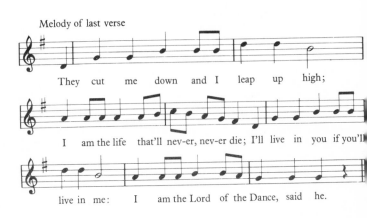

They cut me down and I leap up high;

I am the life that'll nev-er, nev-er die; I'll live in you if you'll

live in me: I am the Lord of the Dance, said he.

Lord of the Dance

Solo
I danced in the morning
    when the world was begun,
And I danced in the moon
    and the stars and the sun,
And I came down from heaven
    and I danced on the earth;
At Bethlehem
    I had my birth:

All
Dance, then, wherever you may be;
I am the Lord of the Dance, said he,
And I'll lead you all, wherever you
    may be,
And I'll lead you all in the dance,
    said he.

2

I danced for the scribe
    and the pharisee,
But they would not dance
    and they wouldn't follow me;
I danced for the fishermen,
    for James and John;
They came with me
    and the dance went on:

3

I danced on the Sabbath
    and I cured the lame:
The holy people
    said it was a shame.
They whipped and they stripped
    and they hung me high,
And they left me there
    on a cross to die:

4

I danced on a Friday
    when the sky turned black;
It's hard to dance
    with the devil on your back.
They buried my body
    and they thought I'd gone;
But I am the dance
    and I still go on:

5

They cut me down
    and I leap up high;
I am the life
    that'll never, never die;
I'll live in you
    if you'll live in me:
I am the Lord
    of the Dance, said he:

SYDNEY CARTER (b. 1915)

Brotherhood

In Christ there is no east or west,
in him no south or north,
But one great fellowship of love
throughout the whole wide earth.

2

In him shall true hearts everywhere
their high communion find;
His service is the golden cord,
close binding all mankind.

3

Join hands, then, brothers of the faith,
whate'er your race may be;
Who serves my Father as a son
is surely kin to me.

4

In Christ now meet both east and west,
in him meet south and north;
All Christlike souls are one in him,
throughout the whole wide earth.

JOHN OXENHAM* (1852–1941)

Alternative Tune: *Ellacombe* (A.M.R. 132; E.H. 137; S.P. 193; C.P. 230)

The World's Need

In humble gratitude, O God,
  we bring our best to thee,
To serve thy cause and share thy love
  with all humanity.
O thou who gavest us thyself
  in Jesus Christ thy Son,
Teach us to give ourselves each day
  until life's work is done.

2

A world in need now summons us
  to labour, love, and give;
To make our life an offering
  to God, that man may live;
The Church of Christ is calling us
  to make the dream come true:
A world redeemed by Christlike love,
  all life in Christ made new.

FRANK VON CHRISTIERSON* (b. 1900)

Son of Man

Jesus, good above all other,
gentle child of gentle mother,
in a stable born our brother,
    give us grace to persevere.

2

Jesus, cradled in a manger,
for us facing every danger,
living as a homeless stranger,
    make we thee our King most dear.

3

Jesus, for thy people dying,
risen Master, death defying,
Lord in heaven, thy grace supplying,
    keep us to thy presence near.

4

Jesus, who our sorrows bearest,
all our thoughts and hopes thou sharest,
thou to man the truth declarest;
    help us all thy truth to hear.

5

Lord, in all our doings guide us;
pride and hate shall ne'er divide us;
we'll go on with thee beside us,
    and with joy we'll persevere.

PERCY DEARMER (1867–1936)
partly based on J. M. Neale (1818–66)

46 Buckland 7 7.7 7.   L. G. Hayne (1836–83)

Christ in Us

Jesus, humble was your birth,
when you came from heaven to earth;
    every day, in all we do,
    make us humble, Lord, like you.

2

Jesus, strong to help and heal,
showing that your love is real;
    every day in all we do,
    make us strong and kind like you.

3

Jesus, when you were betrayed,
still you trusted God and prayed;
    every day in all we do,
    help us trust and pray like you.

4

Jesus, risen from the dead,
with us always, as you said;
    every day in all we do,
    help us live and love like you.

PATRICK APPLEFORD* (b. 1924)

Melody by J. H. Knecht (1752–1817)

Unity

Jesus, Lord, we look to thee,
let us in thy name agree:
    show thyself the Prince of Peace;
    bid all strife for ever cease.

2

Make us of one heart and mind,
courteous, pitiful, and kind,
    lowly, meek in thought and word,
    altogether like our Lord.

3

Let us for each other care,
each the other's burden bear;
    to thy Church the pattern give,
    show how true believers live.

4

Still our fellowship increase,
knit us in the bond of peace:
    join our new-born spirits, join
    each to each, and all to thine.

5

Free from anger and from pride,
let us thus in God abide;
    all the depths of love express,
    all the heights of holiness.

Cento from CHARLES WESLEY* (1707–88)

48 St. Etheldreda C.M.   Thomas Turton (1780–1864)

Our Brother's Need

Jesus, my Lord, how rich thy grace,
  how fair thy bounties shine!
What can my poverty bestow,
  when all the worlds are thine?

2

But thou hast needy brethren here,
  the partners of thy grace,
And wilt confess their humble names
  before thy Father's face.

3

In them thou may'st be clothed and fed,
  and visited and cheered,
And in their accents of distress
  the Saviour's voice is heard.

4

Thy face with reverence and with love
  I in thy poor would see;
O let me rather beg my bread,
  than hold it back from thee.

PHILIP DODDRIDGE★ (1702–51)

(Two bars organ introduction before verse 1)

vv. 1-4 | last verse

Following Christ

Jesus our Lord, our King and our God,
   ruling in might and love,
All power on earth is given to you,
   you are our King above;
     Help us to use the power you give,
     Humbly to order how men live.
Lord, we are called to follow you;
This we ask strength to do.

Jesus our Lord, and humblest of Priests,
   doing your Father's will;
Suffering servant, working with men,
   your work continues still.
     Help us to offer in our prayer,
     All of our work and service here.
Lord, we are called to follow you;
This we ask strength to do.

3

Jesus our Lord, and Shepherd of men,
   caring for human needs;
Feeding the hungry, healing the sick,
   showing your love in deeds;
     Help us in your great work to share;
     People in want still need your care.
Lord, we are called to follow you;
This we ask strength to do.

4

Jesus our Lord, and Prophet of God,
   preaching his mighty plan,
You are the Way, the Truth and the Life,
   teaching the mind of man;
     Help us in all our words to show
     You are the truth men need to know.
Lord, we are called to follow you;
This we ask strength to do.

5

Jesus our Lord, our God and our Priest,
   Prophet and Shepherd-King,
Yours is the kingdom, glory and power,
   yours is the praise we sing.
     Leader of men, you show the way
     We are to follow day by day.
Glorious God, we follow you;
This you give strength to do.

PATRICK APPLEFORD (b. 1924)

Sinners' Friend

Jesus, whose all-redeeming love
   no penitent did scorn,
Who didst the stain of guilt remove,
   till hope anew was born;

2

To thee, physician of the soul,
   the lost, the outcast, came;
Thou didst restore and make them whole,
   unburdened of their shame.

3

'Twas love, thy love, their bondage brake,
   whose fetters sin had bound;
For faith to love did answer make,
   and free forgiveness found.

4

Thou didst rebuke the scornful pride
   that called thee 'sinners' friend';
Thy mercy as thy Father's wide,
   God's mercy without end.

5

Jesus, that pardoning grace to find,
   I too would come to thee;
O merciful to all mankind,
   be merciful to me.

G. W. Briggs* (1875–1959)

Lindeman 8 7. 8 7. 8 8 7.   Ludwig Matthias Lindeman (1812–87)

Alternative Tune: *Luther* (A.M.R. 366; E.H. 4; S.P. 672; C.P. 250)

The Justice of God

Lo, in the wilderness a voice
   'Make straight the way' is crying:
When men are turning from the light,
   and hope and love seem dying,
The prophet comes to make us clean:
'There standeth one you have not seen,
   whose voice you are denying'.

2

God, give us grace to hearken now
   to those who come to warn us;
Give sight and strength, that we may kill
   the vices that have torn us;
Lest love professed should disappear
In creeds of hate, contempt, and fear,
   that crash and overturn us.

3

When from the vineyard cruel men
   cast out the heavenly powers,
And Christendom denies its Lord,
   the world in ruin cowers.
Now come, O God, in thy great might!
Unchanged, unchanging is thy right,
   unswayed thy justice towers.

PERCY DEARMER (1867–1936)

Into the World

Lord, as we rise to leave the shell of worship,
called to the risk of unprotected living,
willing to be at one with all your people,
    we ask for courage.

2

For all the strain with living interwoven,
for the demands each day will make upon us,
and all the love we owe the world around us,
    Lord, make us cheerful.

3

Give us an eye for openings to serve you,
make us alert when calm is interrupted,
ready and wise to use the unexpected;
    sharpen our insight.

4

Lift from our life the blanket of convention,
give us the nerve to lose our life to others,
lead on your church through death to resurrection,
    Lord of all ages.

FRED KAAN (b. 1929)

Peter Cutts (b. 1937)

Make us One

Lord Christ, the Father's mighty Son,
Whose work upon the cross was done
    all men to receive,
Make all our scattered churches one,
    that the world may believe.

2

To make us one your prayers were said,
To make us one you broke the bread
    for all to receive;
Its pieces scatter us instead:
    how can others believe?

3

Lord Christ, forgive us, make us new!
What our designs could never do
    your love can achieve.
Our prayers, our work, we bring to you,
    that the world may believe.

4

We will not question or refuse
The way you work, the means you choose,
    the pattern you weave;
But reconcile our warring views,
    that the world may believe.

BRIAN WREN (b. 1936)

The Reign of Love

Lord Christ, when first thou cam'st to men,
  upon a cross they bound thee,
And mocked thy saving kingship then
  by thorns with which they crowned thee:
And still our wrongs may weave thee now
New thorns to pierce that steady brow,
  and robe of sorrow round thee.

2

New advent of the love of Christ,
  shall we again refuse thee,
Till in the night of hate and war
  we perish as we lose thee?
From old unfaith our souls release
To seek the kingdom of thy peace,
  by which alone we choose thee.

3

O wounded hands of Jesus, build
  in us thy new creation;
Our pride is dust, our vaunt is stilled;
  we wait thy revelation.
O Love that triumphs over loss,
We bring our hearts before thy cross,
  to finish thy salvation.

W. RUSSELL BOWIE (1882–1969)

Caring

Lord Christ, who on thy heart didst bear◡
    the burden of our shame and sin,
And now on high dost stoop to share◡
    the fight without, the fear within;

2

Thy patience cannot know defeat,
    thy pity will not be denied,
Thy loving-kindness still is great,
    thy tender mercies still abide.

3

O brother Man, for this we pray,
    thou brother Man and sovereign Lord,
That we thy brethren, day by day,
    may follow thee and keep thy word;

4

That we may care, as thou hast cared,
    for sick and lame, for deaf and blind,
And freely share, as thou hast shared,
    in all the sorrows of mankind;

5

That ours may be the holy task◡
    to help and bless, to heal and save;
This is the happiness we ask,
    and this the service that we crave.

ARNOLD THOMAS* (1848–1924)

Alternative Tune: *Farley Castle*, 26 (E.H. 217; S.P. 22; C.P. 121)

Our Destiny

Lord God, thou art our maker and our end;
from thee we come and to thee we ascend;
    we have no rest, nor are we ever free
    until we find our joy and peace in thee.

2

We know we are thy sons, and heaven our home,
and yet with laggard steps to prayer we come;
    and, since on others little love we spend,
    we cannot know thy love which has no end.

3

Then to us, Lord, faith, hope, and courage give
to see thy face in Christ and in him live,
    to learn thy love through him who for us died,
    and find his faith by walking at his side.

4

In Christ, our hope and glory, give us light,
and, after life's last sacrifice, full sight;
    in death a new beginning, then with thee
    adoring service, glorious liberty.

J. R. PEACEY (1896–1971)

57 Ach Herr 8 8 8.D.   Melody from Michael Praetorius (1571–1621)

Humility

Lord God, we see thy power displayed
in all the marvels thou hast made
in earth around and sky above;
But nothing that the mind can know,
nor all creation has to show,
can tell the splendour of thy love.

2

When to thy people thou didst come
among the humble was thy home,
and with the poor and simple men;
Nor wealth, nor power, nor majesty,
but wisdom found its way to thee,
and shepherds knelt around thee then.

3

The little fashions of our day
have turned in unbelief away,
and we are in the age of doubt;
Yet still with humble men of heart
and all who know their need thou art,
for such thou never wilt cast out.

DONALD WYNN HUGHES* (1911–67)

Patrick Appleford (b. 1924)

Living Lord

1

Lord Jesus Christ,
you have come to us,
you are one with us,
    Mary's Son;
Cleansing our souls from all their sin,
pouring your love and goodness in;
Jesus, our love for you we sing,
    Living Lord.

*2

Lord Jesus Christ,
now and every day ‿
teach us how to pray,
    Son of God.
You have commanded us to do ‿
this in remembrance, Lord, of you:
into our lives your power breaks
    Living Lord.   through,

3

Lord Jesus Christ,
you have come to us,
born as one of us,
    Mary's Son.
Led out to die on Calvary,
risen from death to set us free,
living Lord Jesus, help us see ‿
    You are Lord.

4

Lord Jesus Christ,
I would come to you,
live my life for you,
    Son of God.
All your commands I know are true,
your many gifts will make me new,
into my life your power breaks through,
    Living Lord.

PATRICK APPLEFORD (b. 1924)

Alternative Tune: *Winchester New* (A.M.R. 2; E.H. 9; S.P. 137; C.P. 122)

The Gospel

Lord Jesus, once you spoke to men
  upon the mountain, in the plain;
O help us listen now, as then,
  and wonder at your words again.

2

We all have secret fears to face,
  our minds and motives to amend;
We seek your truth, we need your grace,
  our living Lord and present Friend.

3

The Gospel speaks; and we receive
  your light, your love, your own command.
O help us live what we believe
  in daily work of heart and hand.

H. C. A. GAUNT (1902–83)

Self-giving

Lord of all good, our gifts we bring to thee;
  use them thy holy purpose to fulfil:
Tokens of love and pledges they shall be
  that our whole life is offered to thy will.

2

We give our mind to understand thy ways,
  hands, eyes, and voice to serve thy great design;
Heart with the flame of thine own love ablaze,
  till for thy glory all our powers combine.

3

Father, whose bounty all creation shows,
  Christ, by whose willing sacrifice we live,
Spirit, from whom all life in fulness flows,
  to thee with grateful hearts ourselves we give.

ALBERT F. BAYLY (1901-84)

61 Miniver   10 11. 11 12.   Cyril Taylor (b. 1907)

Alternative Tune: *Slane*, 62 (S.P. 565; C.P. 432)

Our Life in His Hands

1

Lord of all hopefulness, Lord of all joy,
whose trust, ever childlike, no cares
       could destroy,
  Be there at our waking, and give us,
       we pray,
    your bliss in our hearts, Lord,
      at the break of the day.

2

Lord of all eagerness, Lord of all fait[h,]
whose strong hands were skilled at th[e]
       plane and the lathe,
  Be there at our labours, and give u[s]
       we pray,
    your strength in our hearts, Lord,
      at the noon of the day.

3

Lord of all kindliness, Lord of all grace,
your hands swift to welcome, your arms to
       embrace,
  Be there at our homing, and give us,
       we pray,
    your love in our hearts, Lord,
      at the eve of the day.

4

Lord of all gentleness, Lord of all calm,
whose voice is contentment, whose presence
       is balm,
  Be there at our sleeping, and give us,
       we pray,
    your peace in our hearts, Lord,
      at the end of the day.

                              JAN STRUTHER (1901–1953)

Self-giving

Lord of all power, I give you my will,
in joyful obedience your tasks to fulfil.
    Your bondage is freedom, your service is song,
    and, held in your keeping, my weakness is strong.

2

Lord of all wisdom, I give you my mind,
rich truth that surpasses man's knowledge to find.
    What eye has not seen and what ear has not heard
    is taught by your Spirit and shines from your Word.

3

Lord of all bounty, I give you my heart;
I praise and adore you for all you impart:
    Your love to inspire me, your counsel to guide,
    your presence to cheer me, whatever betide.

4

Lord of all being, I give you my all;
if e'er I disown you I stumble and fall;
    But, sworn in glad service your word to obey,
    I walk in your freedom to the end of the way.

JACK C. WINSLOW* (1882–1974)

63

Lingwood   8 7.8 7.8 7.   C. Armstrong Gibbs (1889–1960)

Obiit   8 7.8 7.8 7.   Walter Parratt (1841–1924)

Alternative Tune: *Rhuddlan* (A.M.R. 556; E.H. 423; S.P. 552; C.P. 563)

For Church and Nation

Lord of lords and King eternal,
  down the years in wondrous ways
You have blessed our land and guided,
  leading us through darkest days.
For your rich and faithful mercies,
  Lord, accept our thankful praise.

2

Speak to us and every nation,
  bid our jarring discords cease;
To the starving and the homeless
  bid us bring a full release;
And on all this earth's sore turmoil
  breathe the healing of your peace.

3

Love that binds us all together
  be upon the Church outpoured;
Shame our pride and quell our factions,
  smite them with your Spirit's sword;
Till the world, our love beholding,
  claims your power and calls you Lord.

4

Brace the wills of all your people
  who in every land and race
Know the secrets of your kingdom,
  share the treasures of your grace;
Till the summons of your Spirit
  wakes new life in every place.

5

Saviour, by your mighty Passion
  once you turned sheer loss to gain,
Wresting in your risen glory
  victory from your cross and pain;
Now in us be dead and risen,
  in us triumph, live, and reign.

JACK C. WINSLOW* (1882–1974)

As Hymnodus Sacer (Leipzig, 1625)

The World's Need

Lord, save thy world; in bitter need
   thy children lift their cry to thee;
We wait thy liberating deed
   to signal hope and set us free.

2

Lord, save thy world; our souls are bound
   in iron chains of fear and pride;
High walls of ignorance around
   our faces from each other hide.

3

Lord, save thy world; we strive in vain
   to save ourselves without thine aid;
What skill and science slowly gain,
   is soon to evil ends betrayed.

4

Lord, save thy world; but thou hast sent
   the Saviour whom we sorely need;
For us his tears and blood were spent,
   that from our bonds we might be freed.

5

Then save us now, by Jesus' power,
   and use the lives thy love sets free,
To bring at last the glorious hour
   when all men find thy liberty.

ALBERT F. BAYLY (1901-84)

65   Lanteglos   8 8.4.   John Dykes Bower (1905–81)

Adoration

Lord that descendedst, Holy Child,
Dwelling amongst us, Word of God,
Thee we adore.

2

Jesus our Gospel, Way and Truth,
Master and Lover, Light and Life,
Thee we adore.

3

Saviour uplifted, Man for men,
Shamèd and slaughtered, Lamb of God,
Thee we adore.

4

Christ the immortal Risen Lord,
Christ that ascended, King of kings,
Thee we adore.

5

Throned in the highest, Very Man,
Alpha, Omega, God of God,
Thee we adore.

6

Lord ever-blessèd, God most high,
Lord ever-blessèd, God with us,
Thee we adore.

ERIC MILNER-WHITE (1884–1963)

66

Godmanstone 8 8 8.4. Cyril Taylor (b. 1907)

Solo (or group of voices)

All

Es ist kein Tag 8 8 8.4. Melody by J. D. Meyer
(Geistliche Seelen-Freud, 1692)

Men Born Blind

Lord, we are blind; the world of sight
   is as a shadow in the dark.
Yet we have eyes; Lord, give us light
   that we may see.

2

Lord, we are blind; the world around
   confuses us, although we see.
In Christ the pattern is refound;
   he sets us free.

3

Lord, we are blind; our sight, our life
   by our own efforts cannot be.
Breathe on our clay and touch our eyes;
   we would serve thee.

DAVID EDGE (b. 1932)

67 Camden   Melody by Sydney Carter (b. 1915)

Stand-ing in the rain, Knock-ing on the wind-ow, Knock-ing on the wind-ow on a Christ-mas Day.

There he is a-gain, Knock-ing on the wind-ow, Knock-ing on the wind-ow in the same old way.

Solo
No use knocking on the window,
There is nothing we can do, sir;
All the beds are booked already,
There is nothing left for you, sir:

All   *Standing in the rain,*
          Knocking on the window,
          Knocking on the window
             On a Christmas Day.
          There he is again,
          Knocking on the window,
          Knocking on the window
             In the same old way.

2

No use knocking on the window,
Some are lucky, some are not, sir.
We are Christian men and women,
But we're keeping what we've got, sir:

3

No, we haven't got a manger,
No, we haven't got a stable.
We are Christian men and women
Always willing, never able:

4

Jesus Christ has gone to heaven;
One day he'll be coming back, sir.
In this house he will be welcome,
But we hope he won't be black, sir:

5

Wishing you a merry Christmas
We will now go back to bed, sir.
Till you woke us with your knocking
We were sleeping like the dead, sir:

SYDNEY CARTER (b. 1915)

Truth and Light

Not far beyond the sea, nor high
Above the heavens, but very nigh
    thy voice, O God, is heard.
For each new step of faith we take
Thou hast more truth and light to break
    forth from thy Holy Word.

2

Rooted and grounded in thy love,
With saints on earth and saints above
    we join in full accord.
To grasp the breadth, length, depth, and height,
The crucified and risen might
    of Christ, the Incarnate Word.

3

Help us to press toward that mark,
And, though our vision now is dark,
    to live by what we see.
So, when we see thee face to face,
Thy truth and light our dwelling-place
    for evermore shall be.

GEORGE B. CAIRD (1917–84)

C. Steggall (1826–1905)

The New Life

Now is eternal life,
　if ris'n with Christ we stand,
In him to life reborn,
　and holden in his hand;
No more we fear death's ancient dread,
In Christ arisen from the dead.

2

Man long in bondage lay,
　brooding o'er life's brief span;
Was it, O God, for naught,
　for naught, thou madest man?
Thou art our hope, our vital breath;
Shall hope undying end in death?

3

And God, the living God,
　stooped down to man's estate;
By death destroying death,
　Christ opened wide life's gate.
He lives, who died; he reigns on high;
Who lives in him shall never die.

4

Unfathomed love divine,
　reign thou within my heart;
From thee nor depth nor height,
　nor life nor death can part;
My life is hid in God with thee,
Now and through all eternity.

G. W. Briggs (1875–1959)

The Sacrament of Care

Now let us from this table rise,
  renewed in body, mind, and soul;
With Christ we die and live again,
  his selfless love has made us whole.

2

With minds alert, upheld by grace,
  to spread the Word in speech and deed,
We follow in the steps of Christ,
  at one with man in hope and need.

3

To fill each human house with love,
  it is the sacrament of care;
The work that Christ began to do
  we humbly pledge ourselves to share.

4

Then give us courage, Father God,
  to choose again the pilgrim way,
And help us to accept with joy‿
  the challenge of tomorrow's day.

FRED KAAN (b. 1929)

71 Llangloffan 7 6.8 6.D. Welsh Hymn Melody

Christ Crucified Today

1
O crucified Redeemer,
  whose life-blood we have spilt,
To thee we raise our guilty hands,
  and humbly own our guilt.
Today we see thy Passion
  spread open to our gaze;
The crowded street, the country lane,
  its Calvary displays.

2
Wherever love is outraged,
  wherever hope is killed,
Where man still wrongs his brother man,
  thy Passion is fulfilled.
We see thy tortured body,
  we see the wounds that bleed,
Where brotherhood hangs crucified,
  nailed to the cross of greed.

3
We hear thy cry of anguish,
  we see thy life outpoured,
Where battlefield runs red with blood,
  our brothers' blood, O Lord.
And in that bloodless battle,
  the fight for daily bread,
Where might is right and self is king,
  we see thy thorn-crowned head.

4
The groaning of creation,
  wrung out by pain and care,
The anguish of a million hearts
  that break in dumb despair;
O crucified Redeemer,
  these are thy cries of pain;
O may they break our selfish hearts,
  and love come in to reign.

TIMOTHY REES* (1874–1939)

The Day of God

O Day of God, draw nigh
in beauty and in power,
Come with thy timeless judgment now
to match our present hour.

2

Bring to our troubled minds,
uncertain and afraid,
The quiet of a steadfast faith,
calm of a call obeyed.

3

Bring justice to our land,
that all may dwell secure,
And finely build for days to come
foundations that endure.

4

Bring to our world of strife
thy sovereign word of peace,
That war may haunt the earth no more
and desolation cease.

5

O Day of God, draw nigh;
as at creation's birth
Let there be light again, and set
thy judgments in the earth.

R. B. Y. Scott (b. 1899)

73 St. Petersburg 8 8.8 8.8 8. D. S. Bortnianski (1752–1825)

The Healing God

O God, by whose almighty plan
First order out of chaos stirred,
And life, progressive at your word,
Matured through nature up to man;
   Grant us in light and love to grow,
   Your sovereign truth to seek and know.

2

O Christ, whose touch unveiled the blind,
Whose presence warmed the lonely soul;
Your love made broken sinners whole,
Your faith cast devils from the mind.
   Grant us your faith, your love, your care
   To bring to sufferers everywhere.

3

O Holy Spirit, by whose grace
Our skills abide, our wisdom grows,
In every healing work disclose
New paths to probe, new thoughts to trace.
   Grant us your wisest way to go
   In all we think, or speak, or do.

H. C. A. Gaunt (1902–83)

74 Melita 8 8.8 8.8 8. J. B. Dykes (1823–76)

Our Homes

O God in heaven, whose loving plan
ordained for us our parents' care,
And, from the time our life began,
the shelter of a home to share;
 Our Father, on the homes we love
 Send down thy blessing from above.

2

May young and old together find
in Christ the Lord of every day,
That fellowship our homes may bind
in joy and sorrow, work and play.
 Our Father, on the homes we love
 Send down thy blessing from above.

3

The sins that mar our homes forgive;
from all self-seeking set us free;
Parents and children, may we live
in glad obedience to thee.
 Our Father, on the homes we love
 Send down thy blessing from above.

4

O Father, in our homes preside,
their duties shared as in thy sight;
In kindly ways be thou our guide,
on mirth and trouble shed thy light.
 Our Father, on the homes we love
 Send down thy blessing from above.

HUGH MARTIN* (1890–1964)

M. B. Foster (1851–1922)

For Those Who Heal

O God, whose will is life and good
    for all of mortal breath,
Unite in bonds of brotherhood
    all those who fight with death.

2

Make strong their hands and hearts and wills
    to drive disease afar,
To battle with the body's ills,
    and wage thy holy war.

3

Where'er they heal the sick and blind,
    Christ's love may they proclaim;
Make known the good Physician's mind,
    and prove the Saviour's name.

4

Before them set thy holy will,
    that they, with heart and soul,
To thee may consecrate their skill,
    and make the sufferer whole.

H. D. RAWNSLEY* (1851–1920)

76

Sancta Civitas   8 6.8 6.8 6.   Herbert Howells (1892–1983)

(Organ)

SECOND TUNE

Morning Song   8 6.8 6.8 6.   Melody from *The Union Harmony*
(Virginia, 1848)

The City of God

O Holy City, seen of John,
   where Christ, the Lamb, doth reign,
Within whose four-square walls shall
     come
   no night, nor need, nor pain,
And where the tears are wiped from eyes
   that shall not weep again.

2

O shame to us who rest content
   while lust and greed for gain
In street and shop and tenement
   wring gold from human pain,
And bitter lips in blind despair
   cry, 'Christ hath died in vain'.

3

Give us, O God, the strength to build
   the City that hath stood
Too long a dream, whose laws are love,
   whose ways are brotherhood,
And where the sun that shineth is
   God's grace for human good.

4

Already in the mind of God
   that City riseth fair:
Lo, how its splendour challenges
   the souls that greatly dare:
Yea, bids us seize the whole of life
   and build its glory there.

W. RUSSELL BOWIE (1882–1969)

suggested by St. John's vision in Revelation 21

Offertory

O holy Father, God most dear,
behold us round thy altar here,
Accept for sacrifice, we pray,
the common food we here display.
　　For bread set forth, for wine outpoured
　　We bless thee, all-creating Lord.

2

O Christ, who at the supper-board
took bread and wine and spoke the word,
And in that solemn paschal meal
gave Flesh and Blood our wound to heal;
　　For man redeemed, for life restored,
　　We bless thee, all-creating Word.

3

O Holy Spirit, be thou nigh
this bread and cup to sanctify,
That, eating of the Food unpriced,
we form one body, one in Christ.
　　Redeemed, restored in unity,
　　We bless thee, Holy Trinity.

G. A. TOMLINSON (b. 1906)

God's Age-long Plan

O Lord of every shining constellation
    that wheels in splendour through the midnight sky,
Grant us your Spirit's true illumination
    to read the secrets of your work on high.

2

You, Lord, have made the atom's hidden forces,
    your laws its mighty energies fulfil;
Teach us, to whom you give such rich resources,
    in all we use, to serve your holy will.

3

O Life, awaking life in cell and tissue,
    from flower to bird, from beast to brain of man;
Help us to trace, from birth to final issue,
    the sure unfolding of your age-long plan.

4

You, Lord, have stamped your image on your creatures,
    and, though they mar that image, love them still;
Lift up our eyes to Christ, that in his features
    we may discern the beauty of your will.

5

Great Lord of nature, shaping and renewing,
    you made us more than nature's sons to be;
You help us tread, with grace our souls enduing,
    the road to life and immortality.

ALBERT F. BAYLY * (1901-84)

79 Surrey 8 8.8 8.8 8.

Henry Carey (c. 1690–1743)

Walking by Faith

1

O Lord, we long to see your face,
to know you risen from the grave,
But we have missed the joy and grace
of seeing you, as others have.
    Yet in your company we'll wait,
    And we shall see you, soon or late.

2

O Lord, we do not know the way,
nor clearly see the path ahead;
So often, therefore, we delay
and doubt your power to raise the dead.
    Yet with you we will firmly stay;
    You are the Truth, the Life, the Way.

3

We find it hard, Lord, to believe;
all habit makes us want to prove;
We would with eye and hand percei
the truth and person whom we love.
    Yet, as in fellowship we meet,
    You come yourself each one to gr

4

You come to us, our God, our Lord
you do not show your hands and sid
But faith has its more blest reward;
in love's assurance we confide.
    Now we believe, that we may kno
    And in that knowledge daily grow

J. R. PEACEY (1896–197

English Traditional Melody

The Name Above Every Name

1

O sing a song of Bethlehem,
 of shepherds watching there,
And of the news that came to them
 from angels in the air:
The light that shone on Bethlehem
 fills all the world today;
Of Jesus' birth and peace on earth
 the angels sing alway.

2

O sing a song of Nazareth,
 of sunny days of joy,
O sing of fragrant flowers' breath
 and of the sinless Boy:
For now the flowers of Nazareth
 in every heart may grow;
Now spreads the fame of his dear
  name
 on all the winds that blow.

3

O sing a song of Galilee,
 of lake and woods and hill,
Of him who walked upon the sea
 and bade its waves be still:
For though, like waves on Galilee,
 dark seas of trouble roll,
When faith has heard the Master's word,
 falls peace upon the soul.

4

O sing a song of Calvary,
 its glory and dismay;
Of him who hung upon the tree,
 and took our sins away:
For he who died on Calvary
 is risen from the grave,
And Christ our Lord, by heaven adored,
 is mighty now to save.

LOUIS F. BENSON (1855–1930)

Solo (or a few voices)

Lighten our Darkness

Peter feared the Cross for himself and his Master;
Peter tempted Jesus to turn and go back.
      O Lord, have mercy,
      Lighten our darkness.
      We've all been tempters,
      Our light is black.

*2

Judas loved his pride and rejected his Master;
Judas turned a traitor and lost his way back.
      O Lord, have mercy,
      Lighten our darkness.
      We've all been traitors,
      Our light is black.

Peter, James and John fell asleep when their Master
asked them to be praying a few paces back.
> *O Lord, have mercy,*
> *Lighten our darkness.*
> *We've all been sleeping,*
> *Our light is black.*

4

Peter, vexed and tired, thrice denied his own Master;
said he never knew him, to stop a girl's clack.
> *O Lord, have mercy,*
> *Lighten our darkness.*
> *We've all denied you,*
> *Our light is black.*

5

Twelve all ran away and forsook their dear Master;
left him lonely prisoner, a lamb in wolves' pack.
> *O Lord, have mercy,*
> *Lighten our darkness.*
> *We've all been failures,*
> *Our light is black.*

*6

Pilate asked the crowd to set free their good Master.
'Crucify', they shouted, 'we don't want him back!'
> *O Lord, have mercy,*
> *Lighten our darkness.*
> *We crucified you,*
> *Our light is black.*

7

We have watched the Cross and we've scoffed at the Master;
thought the safe way better and tried our own tack.
> *O Lord, have mercy,*
> *Lighten our darkness.*
> *We've all reviled you,*
> *Our light is black.*

EMILY CHISHOLM (b. 1910)

82 Bunessan 5 5. 5 4. D.   Old Gaelic Melody

Bread for the World

1

Praise and thanksgiving,
Father, we offer,
for all things living,
   thou madest good;
     harvest of sown fields,
     fruits of the orchard,
     hay from the mown fields,
     blossom and wood.

2

Bless thou the labour,
we bring to serve thee,
that with our neighbour,
   we may be fed.
     Sowing or tilling,
     we would work with thee;
     harvesting, milling,
     for daily bread.

3

Father, providing,
food for thy children,
thy wisdom guiding
   teaches us share
     one with another,
     so that rejoicing
     with us, our brother,
     may know thy care.

4

Then will thy blessing,
reach every people;
all men confessing,
   thy gracious hand.
     Where thy will reigneth
     no man will hunger:
     thy love sustaineth;
     fruitful the land.

ALBERT F. BAYLY (1901-84)

83 Evangelists   8 8 7.D.   Adapted from J. S. Bach's version of a chorale
(Alles ist an Gottes Segen)   by J. Löhner (1691) and others

Into the World

Praise the Lord, rise up rejoicing,
Worship, thanks, devotion voicing:
   glory be to God on high!
Christ, your Cross and Passion sharing,
By this Eucharist declaring
   yours the eternal victory.

2

Scattered flock, one Shepherd sharing,
Lost and lonely, one voice hearing,
   ears are open to your word;
By your Blood new life receiving,
In your Body firm, believing,
   we are yours, and you the Lord.

3

Send us forth alert and living,
Sins forgiven, wrongs forgiving,
   in your Spirit strong and free.
Finding love in all creation,
Bringing peace in every nation,
   may we faithful followers be.

H. C. A. GAUNT (1902–83)

The Gospel

Praise we now the Word of grace;
May our hearts its truth embrace:
From its pages may we hear
Christ our Teacher, speaking clear.

2

May the Gospel of the Lord
Everywhere be spread abroad,
That the world around may own
Christ as King, and Christ alone.

S. N. SEDGWICK* (1872–1941)

5   Falcon Street (Silver Street)   S.M.

Late form of melody by
Isaac Smith (c. 1770)

Alternative Tune: *Carlisle* (A.M.R. 362; E.H. 190; S.P. 458; C.P. 114)

Service

Rise up, O men of God;
Have done with lesser things;
    Give heart and soul and mind and strength
To serve the King of kings.

2

Rise up, O men of God;
His kingdom tarries long;
    Bring in the day of brotherhood,
And end the night of wrong.

3

Rise up, O men of God;
The Church for you doth wait:
    Her strength unequal to her task;
Rise up, and make her great.

4

Lift high the Cross of Christ;
Tread where his feet have trod;
    As brothers of the Son of Man
Rise up, O men of God.

W. P. MERRILL (1867–1954)

Alternative Tune: *Truro* (A.M.R. 220; E.H. 420; S.P. 337; C.P. 57)

Magnificat Now

Sing we a song of high revolt;
make great the Lord, his name exalt:
  sing we the song that Mary sang
  of God at war with human wrong.

2

Sing we of him who deeply cares
and still with us our burden bears;
  he, who with strength the proud disowns,
  brings down the mighty from their thrones.

3

By him the poor are lifted up;
he satisfies with bread and cup
  the hungry men of many lands;
  the rich are left with empty hands.

4

He calls us to revolt and fight
with him for what is just and right,
  to sing and live Magnificat
  in crowded street and council flat.

FRED KAAN (b. 1929)

Son of Man

1
Son of the Lord Most High,
    who gave the worlds their birth,
He came to live and die
    the Son of Man on earth:
        In Bethlem's stable born was he,
        And humbly bred in Galilee.

2
Born in so low estate,
    schooled in a workman's trade,
Not with the high and great
    his home the Highest made:
        But labouring by his brethren's side,
        Life's common lot he glorified.

3
Then, when his hour was come,
    he heard his Father's call:
And leaving friends and home,
    he gave himself for all:
        Glad news to bring, the lost to find;
        To heal the sick, the lame, the blind.

4
Toiling by night and day,
    himself oft burdened sore,
Where hearts in bondage lay,
    himself their burden bore:
        Till, scorned by them he died to save,
        Himself in death, as life, he gave.

5
O lowly Majesty,
    lofty in lowliness.
Blest Saviour, who am I
    to share thy blessedness?
        Yet thou hast called me, even me,
        Servant divine, to follow thee.

                                        G. W. BRIGGS (1875–1959)

Into the World

Strengthen for service, Lord, the hands
　　that holy things have taken;
Let ears that now have heard thy songs
　　to clamour never waken.

2

Lord, may the tongues which 'Holy' sang
　　keep free from all deceiving;
The eyes which saw thy love be bright,
　　thy blessèd hope perceiving.

3

The feet that tread thy holy courts
　　from light do thou not banish;
The bodies by thy Body fed
　　with thy new life replenish.

Ascr. to Ephraim the Syrian (*c.* 306–73)
tr. C. W. HUMPHREYS (1841–1921)
and PERCY DEARMER (1867–1936)

89 Woodlands 10 10. 10 10.   Walter Greatorex (1877–1949)

Magnificat

Tell out, my soul, the greatness of the Lord:
  unnumbered blessings, give my spirit voice;
Tender to me the promise of his word;
  in God my Saviour shall my heart rejoice.

2

Tell out, my soul, the greatness of his name:
  make known his might, the deeds his arm has done;
His mercy sure, from age to age the same;
  his holy name, the Lord, the Mighty One.

3

Tell out, my soul, the greatness of his might:
  powers and dominions lay their glory by;
Proud hearts and stubborn wills are put to flight,
  the hungry fed, the humble lifted high.

4

Tell out, my soul, the glories of his word:
  firm is his promise, and his mercy sure.
Tell out, my soul, the greatness of the Lord
  to children's children and for evermore.

TIMOTHY DUDLEY-SMITH (b. 1926)
based on St. Luke 1, 46–55
in *The New English Bible*

H. P. Allen (1869–1946)

Alternative Tune: *St. Helen* (A.M.R. 400)

The Word of God

1

Thanks to God whose Word was spoken
  in the deed that made the earth.
His the voice that called a nation,
  his the fires that tried her worth.
      God has spoken:
  Praise him for his open Word.

2

Thanks to God whose Word incarnate
  glorified the flesh of man.
Deeds and words and death and rising
  tell the grace in heaven's plan.
      God has spoken:
  Praise him for his open Word.

3

Thanks to God whose Word was written
  in the Bible's sacred page,
Record of the revelation
  showing God to every age.
      God has spoken:
  Praise him for his open Word.

4

Thanks to God whose Word is published
  in the tongues of every race.
See its glory undiminished
  by the change of time or place.
      God has spoken:
  Praise him for his open Word.

5

Thanks to God whose Word is answered
  by the Spirit's voice within.
Here we drink of joy unmeasured,
  life redeemed from death and sin.
      God is speaking:
  Praise him for his open Word.

R. T. BROOKS (b. 1918)

91 St. Thomas S.M. Melody by Aaron Williams (1731–76)

The Lord's Day

1

The first day of the week,
His own, in sad despair,
Could not believe for very joy
The risen Lord was there.

2

Now they obeyed his word,
Now shared what Jesus gave,
And, one in him, in breaking bread
Knew what it costs to save.

3

And each day of the week,
And on the Lord's own day,
They walked in Christian liberty
His new and living Way.

4

And on the Lord's own day,
From needless burdens freed,
They kept a Sabbath made for man,
To fit man's inmost need.

5

How soon men forge again
The fetters of their past!
As long as Jesus lives in us,
So long our freedoms last.

6

This day his people meet,
This day his word is sown.
Lord Jesus, show us how to use
This day we call your own.

F. PRATT GREEN (b. 1903)

Race Relations

1

The God who rules this earth
  gave life to every race;
He chose its day of birth,
  the colour of its face;
So none may claim superior grade
Within the family he's made.

2

But sin infects us all,
  distorts the common good;
The universal fall
  corrupts all brotherhood;
So racial pride and colour strife
Spread fear and hate throughout
      man's life.

3

Between the West and East,
  yet neither black nor white
Behold, God's Son released!
  in whom all men unite.
He comes with unrestricted grace
To heal the hearts of every race.

4

That Man alone combines
  all lives within his own;
That Man alone enshrines
  all flesh, all blood, all bone;
That Man accepts all human pain,
That Man breaks death; that Man
      shall reign.

5

To him we bring our praise,
  on him all hopes depend;
Sole Master of our days,
  in him we see the End;
Man's final Lord, God's perfect Son,
In Jesus Christ are all made one.

RICHARD G. JONES (b. 1926)

93 Crimond C.M.   Melody by Jessie S. Irvine (1836–87)

God's Providence

The Lord's my Shepherd, I'll not want;
  he makes me down to lie
In pastures green; he leadeth me
  the quiet waters by.

2

My soul he doth restore again,
  and me to walk doth make
Within the paths of righteousness,
  e'en for his own name's sake.

3

Yea, though I walk through death's dark vale,
  yet will I fear none ill;
For thou art with me, and thy rod
  and staff me comfort still.

4

My table thou hast furnishèd
  in presence of my foes;
My head thou dost with oil anoint,
  and my cup overflows.

5

Goodness and mercy all my life
  shall surely follow me;
And in God's house for evermore
  my dwelling-place shall be.

Psalm 23 in SCOTTISH PSALTER (1650)

Alternative Tune: *Carlisle* (A.M.R. 362; E.H. 190; S.P. 458; C.P. 114)

Lord of Life and Death

The Son of God proclaim,
   the Lord of time and space;
The God who bade the light break forth
   now shines in Jesus' face.

2

He, God's creative Word,
   the Church's Lord and Head,
Here bids us gather as his friends
   and share his wine and bread.

3

The Lord of life and death
   with wond'ring praise we sing;
We break the bread at his command
   and name him God and King.

4

We take this cup in hope;
   for he, who gladly bore
The shameful Cross, is risen again
   and reigns for evermore.

BASIL E. BRIDGE (b. 1927)

95 Maccabaeus   10 11. 11 11. and refrain   G. F. Handel (1685–1759)

Risen with Christ

Thine be the glory, risen, conquering Son,
Endless is the victory thou o'er death hast won;
Angels in bright raiment rolled the stone away,
Kept the folded grave-clothes where thy body lay.

Thine be the glory, risen, conquering Son,
Endless is the victory thou o'er death hast won.

2

Lo, Jesus meets us, risen from the tomb;
Lovingly he greets us, scatters fear and gloom;
Let the Church with gladness hymns of triumph sing,
For her Lord now liveth, death hath lost its sting:

3

No more we doubt thee, glorious Prince of Life;
Life is nought without thee: aid us in our strife;
Make us more than conquerors through thy deathless love;
Bring us safe through Jordan to thy home above:

E. L. Budry (1854–1932)
tr. R. B. Hoyle (1875–1939)

Jeremiah Clarke (c. 1659–1707)

Offertory

Upon thy table, Lord, we place
   these symbols of our work and thine,
Life's food won only by thy grace,
   who giv'st to all the bread and wine.

2

Within these simple things there lie
   the height and depth of human life,
The thought of man, his tears and toil,
   his hopes and fears, his joy and strife.

3

Accept them, Lord; from thee they come:
   we take them humbly at thy hand.
These gifts of thine for higher use
   we offer, as thou dost command.

M. F. C. WILLSON* (1884–1944)

Adapted from a melody by George Gardner
(1853–1925)

Incognito

We find thee, Lord, in others' need,
  we see thee in our brothers;
By loving word and kindly deed
  we serve the Man for Others.

2

We look around and see thy face‿
  disfigured, marred, neglected;
We find thee Lord in every place,
  sought for and unexpected.

3

We offer in simplicity‿
  our loving gift and labour;
And what we do, we do to thee,
  incarnate in our neighbour.

4

We love since we are loved by thee;
  new strength from thee we gather;
And in thy service we shall be‿
  made perfect with each other.

GILES AMBROSE (b. 1912)

William Gardiner, *Sacred Melodies, 1815*

Good News

We have a gospel to proclaim,
   good news for men in all the earth;
The gospel of a Saviour's name:
   we sing his glory, tell his worth.

2

Tell of his birth at Bethlehem
   not in a royal house or hall
But in a stable dark and dim,
   the Word made flesh, a light for all.

3

Tell of his death at Calvary,
   hated by those he came to save,
In lonely suffering on the Cross;
   for all he loved his life he gave.

4

Tell of that glorious Easter morn:
   empty the tomb, for he was free.
He broke the power of death and hell
   that we might share his victory.

5

Tell of his reign at God's right hand,
   by all creation glorified.
He sends his Spirit on his Church
   to live for him, the Lamb who died.

6

Now we rejoice to name him King:
   Jesus is Lord of all the earth.
This gospel-message we proclaim:
   we sing his glory, tell his worth.

EDWARD J. BURNS (b. 1938)

99 Sharpthorne 6 6.6 6.3 3.6. Erik Routley (1917–82)

True Religion

1

What does the Lord require
    for praise and offering?
What sacrifice desire
    or tribute bid you bring?
        Do justly;
        Love mercy;
Walk humbly with your God.

2

Rulers of men, give ear!
    should you not justice know?
Will God your pleading hear,
    while crime and cruelty grow?
        Do justly;
        Love mercy;
Walk humbly with your God.

3

Masters of wealth and trade,
    all you for whom men toil,
Think not to win God's aid,
    if lies your commerce soil.
        Do justly;
        Love mercy;
Walk humbly with your God.

4

Still down the ages ring
    the prophet's stern commands:
To merchant, worker, king,
    he brings God's high demands:
        Do justly;
        Love mercy;
Walk humbly with your God.

5

How shall our life fulfil
    God's law so hard and high?
Let Christ endue our will
    with grace to fortify.
        Then justly,
        In mercy,
We'll humbly walk with God.

ALBERT F. BAYLY* (1901-84)
based on Micah 6, 6–8

Melody by Sydney Carter (b. 1915)

And the creed and the col-our and the

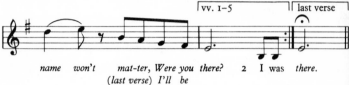

name won't mat-ter, Were you there? 2 I was there.
(last verse) I'll be

Christian Aid

Solo When I needed a neighbour, were you there,
       were you there?
    When I needed a neighbour, were you there?

All   *And the creed and the colour and the name*
       won't matter,
   Were you there?

2

I was hungry and thirsty, were you there,
    were you there?
I was hungry and thirsty, were you there?

3

I was cold, I was naked, were you there,
    were you there?
I was cold, I was naked, were you there?

4

When I needed a shelter, were you there,
    were you there?
When I needed a shelter, were you there?

5

When I needed a healer, were you there,
    were you there?
When I needed a healer, were you there?

6

Wherever you travel, I'll be there,
    I'll be there,
Wherever you travel, I'll be there,

And the creed and the colour and the name
    won't matter,
I'll be there.

SYDNEY CARTER (b. 1915)